anythink

D0821929

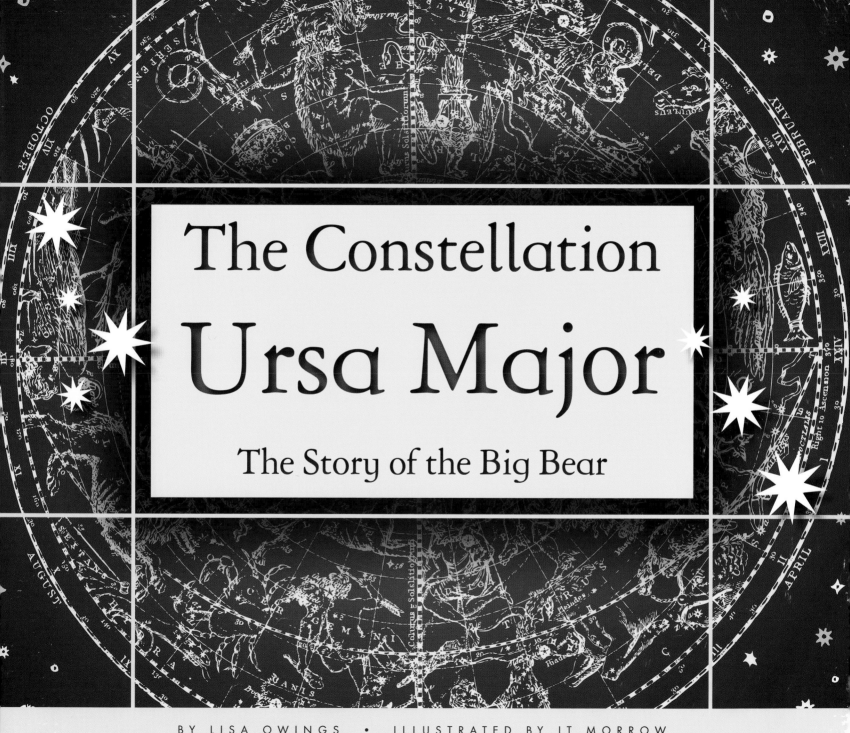

The Constellation
Ursa Major
The Story of the Big Bear

BY LISA OWINGS · ILLUSTRATED BY JT MORROW

The Child's World

Published by The Child's World®
1980 Lookout Drive • Mankato, MN 56003-1705
800-599-READ • www.childsworld.com

Acknowledgments
The Child's World®: Mary Berendes, Publishing Director
Red Line Editorial: Editorial direction and production
The Design Lab: Design

Photographs ©: Sergey Mikhaylov/Shutterstock Images, 5; NASA, 6, 10, 16; Antonio Abrignani/Shutterstock Images, 7; iStockphoto, 9; NASA, ESA and the Hubble Heritage Team STScI/AURA, 11; Neutronman/iStockphoto, 13; De Agostini/Getty Images, 15; North Wind Picture Archives, 17; Library of Congress, 26; Stu Porter/Shutterstock Images, 27

Design elements: Alisafoytik/Dreamstime

ISBN: 9781623234898
LCCN: 2013931332

Printed in the United States of America
Mankato, MN
July, 2013
PA02168

ABOUT THE AUTHOR

Lisa Owings has a degree in English and creative writing from the University of Minnesota. She has written and edited a wide variety of educational books for young people. Lisa lives in Andover, Minnesota, where she can see Ursa Major every night.

ABOUT THE ILLUSTRATOR

JT Morrow has worked as a freelance illustrator for more than 20 years and has won several awards. He also works in graphic design and animation. Morrow lives just south of San Francisco, California, with his wife and daughter.

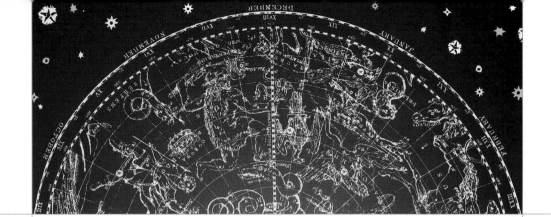

Table of Contents

CHAPTER 1

The Constellation Ursa Major

URSA MINOR

One of the other constellations looks much like Ursa Major, but smaller. This constellation is Ursa Minor, the Little Bear. The Great Bear and the Little Bear keep each other company in the sky.

Many thousands of years ago, people and bears roamed the earth together. Ancient peoples hunted bears. But they also saw that bears were like them. They stood on two legs as people did. These same ancient peoples watched the night sky. They tried to make sense of the shining stars. Slowly the stars began to take shape, as clouds sometimes do. One group of stars looked like a great bear. The star-bear circles the northern skies. It seems to stand sometimes on four legs and sometimes on two.

This constellation is called Ursa Major, the Great Bear.

Many stories are told of how the Great Bear got up in the sky. The Greeks say the bear was once the beautiful huntress Callisto. The mighty god Zeus fell in love with her. But Zeus was married to the goddess Hera. In her jealousy, Hera turned Callisto into a bear. Yet her shape didn't change Zeus's love. He swung Callisto into the sky. There she would be safe from Hera's anger and hunters' arrows.

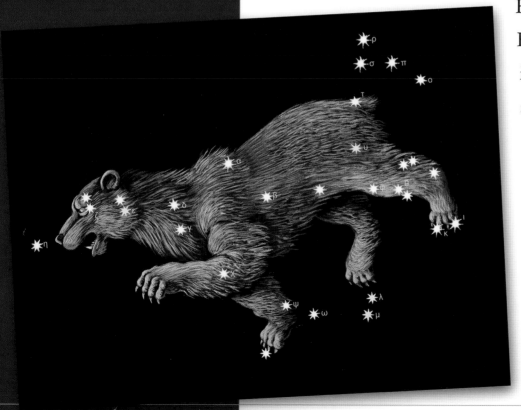

▼ *The Great Bear hunts in the northern skies.*

Stars and Constellations

The stars in our night sky look small. That is because they are so far away. If you could get close to one, you would see a giant ball of brightly burning gas. Some stars are bigger than others. The largest known star is at least 2,000 times the size of our Sun! Some stars also burn brighter than others. Large, bright stars are the easiest to see at night.

Every star in the sky is part of a constellation. These groups of stars form pictures or patterns. They might look like animals or people or tools. Constellations also include the pieces of sky around their stars. Ursa Major makes its home in a large piece of sky. It is the third largest of the 88 constellations.

▼ A space telescope captured this picture of Earth's moon moving in front of the Sun.

▼ This old star map shows many of the constellations.

The Big Dipper and Its Stars

The seven brightest stars of Ursa Major make up the Big Dipper. This group of stars within another group is called an **asterism**. The Big Dipper is the best-known asterism. Its curved handle has three stars. These stars also form the tail of Ursa Major. At the end of the handle is the star Alkaid. It shines brightly in the sky. Mizar and Alcor mark the middle of the handle. We see one star, but actually it's two. The last star in the handle is called Alioth. This is the Big Dipper's brightest star.

Four stars make up the dipper's bowl. The brightest of these four is Dubhe. It sits farthest from the handle. Dubhe marks the back of Ursa Major. Merak is the other star at this end of the dipper. Dubhe and Merak are called the Pointers. A line drawn from Merak through Dubhe points to the

RUNAWAY STARS

The Big Dipper won't always look like a dipper. Two of its stars are slowly moving away from the others. Alkaid's movement will someday give the dipper's handle a sharper curve. The motion of Dubhe will make the bowl of the dipper longer and shallower.

North Star, Polaris. Phecda joins Merak at the bottom of the bowl. The fainter star where the bowl meets the handle is Megrez.

Other Stars in Ursa Major

The other stars in Ursa Major are harder to see. A triangle of stars near the dipper's bowl marks the front part of the bear. The star Muscida serves as its nose. Below the bear's body are three pairs of stars. Each pair marks one of the bear's giant paws. The fourth paw is left to be imagined. Nearby stars reveal Ursa Major's legs.

Galaxies and Nebulae

Not all things that shine in the night sky are stars. Some are **planets** like Earth. Others are whole **galaxies**. Even the closest galaxies are far away from ours. They look like bright blurs through a telescope. Ursa Major is rich in galaxies.

▼ The galaxy M81 forms a beautiful spiral.

▲ *Many stars are born in the galaxy M82.*

M81 is the brightest. It sits above the bear's shoulders. M82 hovers nearby. This galaxy looks like a dove with spread wings.

Above the bear's tail is the pinwheel-shaped galaxy M101.

Nebulae are clouds of dust and gas where stars are born. The Owl Nebula glows faintly within Ursa Major. A large telescope shows how it was named. Its circular cloud has two dark patches. They look like large eyes in an owl's face.

CHAPTER 2

The Origin of the Myth of Ursa Major

Ursa Major is said to be the oldest constellation. No one remembers when these stars became grouped together. It may have happened more than 14,000 years ago. At first, the constellation included only the stars of the Big Dipper. Many people knew it as a wagon or a **plow**. But ancient peoples across Europe, Asia, and North America saw a different pattern. They knew this group of stars as a great bear.

For most, the bowl of the Big Dipper was the bear. The three stars of its handle were fierce hunters.

▶ *Opposite page: People have seen the Big Dipper for thousands of years. Can you find it in this picture?*

They chased the bear forever through the skies. Others saw the whole dipper as a bear. But this bear had a very long tail. It didn't look much like a bear. So **astronomers** made the constellation bigger. That way the bear's tail only looked a little bit too long. This bigger constellation is the modern Ursa Major.

Greek Storytellers and Astronomers

Stories of the star-bear have been told since long before people could write them down. But the Greeks shaped the story told today. The Greek poet Homer wrote of the bear almost 3,000 years ago. He noted that its stars never sank below the **horizon**.

Hesiod was another Greek poet who lived around Homer's time. He was the first known to tell the story of Callisto turning into the Great Bear. Other Greeks and Romans retold the story. Each changed it slightly. Even today, there are many different versions. All end with Zeus placing the she-bear Callisto in the sky.

Greek astronomers knew the bear constellation well. Ptolemy wrote a book about the constellations around 150 AD. In it, he listed the Great Bear. He also wrote about the Little Bear and 46 other groups of stars.

▶ *This medieval tapestry shows Zeus and Callisto falling in love.*

THE OTHER MYTH OF URSA MAJOR
Some ancient Greeks told a different story about Ursa Major. They said she was Adrasteia, a goddess who helped care for the young Zeus. Zeus's father had eaten all his other children. So Zeus's mother hid him in an island cave. Adrasteia and her sister Ida cared for and protected baby Zeus. When he grew up, he set them in the sky as the Great and Little Bears.

Ursa Major in Greek Culture

Gods and goddesses were part of Greeks' everyday life. Zeus was the most powerful god. Many Greeks claimed to be related to him. Callisto's story is especially important to the Greeks who lived in Arcadia. Zeus and Callisto's son, Arcas, is said to be the father of the Arcadians. Through Arcas, they can trace their history back to Zeus.

The Great Bear in History

Many ancient peoples believed bears were special. Some may even have **worshipped** bears. These animals often stood and sometimes walked on their hind legs. When they did, they looked like people. Stories of the close connection between people and bears go back thousands of years. Bears were also prized by hunters. They had good meat and

▲ *Callisto is important enough that one of Jupiter's moons, bottom, was named after her.*

warm fur. It is no surprise these early peoples saw a bear in the night sky.

Ursa Major's brightest stars showed people the way north. In the mid-1800s, slaves in the southern United States used the Big Dipper to help them escape. They called the constellation the Drinking Gourd. They followed it north to freedom. A song called "Follow the Drinking Gourd" describes how they found their way.

▼ People escaping slavery often traveled by night so they could follow the stars.

CHAPTER 3

The Story of Ursa Major

One day, Callisto went hunting in the forest. The beautiful maiden hunted all morning. By noon, she was tired. She went deep into the forest to find a shady place to rest. Callisto carefully set down her bow and **quiver** full of arrows. Then she lay in the soft grass. She used her quiver for a pillow.

Zeus, king of the gods, caught sight of her. The goddess Hera was his wife and queen. But Zeus fell in love with Callisto's beauty. He didn't want to frighten the young huntress. So he took the form of Callisto's dear friend Artemis, the goddess of the hunt.

Callisto woke to find her friend nearby. The two began to talk excitedly. After a while, Zeus could hide no longer. He revealed himself and his true feelings. Callisto was confused. She had promised Artemis that she would never love a man. Nor did she wish for a god's love. But Zeus was very powerful, and Callisto could not refuse him. She became his companion. Soon they had a son together. They called him Arcas.

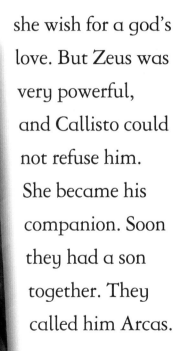

It wasn't long before Hera found out what her husband had done. The queen of gods was wild with jealousy. She quickly found Callisto. Shouting curses, Hera grabbed her by the hair. She dragged the lovely huntress to the ground. Callisto begged the goddess to forgive her. But even as she spoke, dark fur spread down her arms and legs. Callisto's hands grew heavy. Her fingernails curled into sharp claws. Her open mouth showed jaws with yellow, pointed teeth. And finally, her pleading words turned into fearsome growls. Callisto realized in horror what she had become—a bear!

Callisto roamed the forest in fear. The huntress had become the hunted. She fled from her friends' arrows on four legs. Sometimes she forgot she was a bear. When other bears or beasts passed by, she hid. Callisto also missed her son. Hunters had found Arcas in the forest. They brought him to Callisto's father, who raised him as his own.

Years passed. Arcas grew into a young man. He became a skilled hunter, as his mother had been. But he did not remember her. One day Arcas took his spear into the forest. He stalked through the woods, enjoying the hunt. Suddenly he saw a patch of fur through nearby trees. He crept closer. Then he drew back in fright. It was a bear! And it had seen him!

In fact, the bear was staring at him. Arcas did not understand why the beast was behaving so strangely. Why did it not run away? Instead, the bear moved toward him. Its huffs and growls were terrible and threatening. The bear was going to attack! Arcas raised his weapon. He pointed it at the bear's broad chest, ready to strike a deadly blow. He had no way of knowing that this bear was his beloved mother.

Just then, Zeus appeared. He stopped Arcas from throwing his spear. Then he turned the boy into a bear. Now Arcas could recognize his mother. In this form, the two could be together. They would never be apart again.

Zeus grabbed each bear by the tail. Then he swung them high into the heavens. Their tails were stretched out where Zeus had pulled them. But their stars lit up the whole night sky. There they would stay forever, the Great and Little Bears.

Hera's anger once again burned hot. How could her husband give Callisto such an honored place? How dare he make her queen of the night sky! Good thing she was so high, or Hera would have snatched her sparkling crown. The goddess-queen complained to the sea gods. She begged them not to let Callisto or her son bathe in their waters. The sea gods obeyed Hera's request. This is why the Great and Little Bears never dip below the horizon into the ocean's waves.

CHAPTER 4

Ursa Major in Other Cultures

Some Native American tribes saw a bear in Ursa Major's stars. But they told a different story than the Greeks. To them, the bear's tail was not so long. Its three stars were hunters or a hunter and his dogs. Another Native American myth tells of seven brothers and their sister. They climbed into the sky to escape danger. The seven brothers became the stars of the Big Dipper. Their sister

▼ Many cultures saw a bear in Ursa Major, but only some cultures saw the bear's long tail.

▲ Arab stargazers saw the tracks of a leaping gazelle in the stars of Ursa Major.

was the small star close to Mizar called Alcor.

Ancient Egyptians saw Ursa Major's brightest stars as an animal's thigh. In India, the stars of the Big Dipper represent the Seven Sages. Alcor is the wife of one of these wise men. Europeans, Chinese, and many other cultures saw Ursa Major as a chariot or wagon. It rolled around the North Star. Often it was said to belong to a king or other important figure. Arabs told a tale about the pairs of stars in Ursa Major's paws. They called these stars the Three Leaps of the Gazelle. The gazelle left its tracks in the sky as it ran from a hungry lion.

CHAPTER 5

How to Find Ursa Major

Ursa Major can always be seen in northern skies. The Big Dipper is easy to find. Face north. Then look for its seven bright stars. If the night is clear, search next to the dipper's bowl for the bear's nose. Then look for the pairs of stars that mark its paws.

The Great Bear is highest in the sky in the spring. But it is also upside-down. In fall the bear is right-side up but low on the horizon. Some say it is looking for a place to spend the winter. But the Great Bear always spends winters in the sky. In winter and summer, it seems to stand on its hind legs. It is the closest the bear ever gets to human form.

▶ Opposite page: *The Big Dipper's seven stars are bright and easy to find.*

Glossary

asterism (AS-tuh-rih-zem)
An asterism is a well-known group of stars that is smaller than a constellation. The Big Dipper is a famous asterism.

astronomers (uh-STRAW-nuh-murz)
Scientists who study stars and other objects in space are called astronomers. The astronomers discovered a new star.

galaxies (GAL-ax-eez)
Groups of millions or billions of stars form galaxies. Some bright lights in the night sky are galaxies.

horizon (huh-RYE-zun)
The horizon is the line where the ground or water seems to meet the sky. The sun goes below the horizon when it sets.

nebulae (NEB-you-lay)
Nebulae are clouds of gas, dust, and stars in space. You can find nebulae in the constellation Ursa Major.

North Star (north stahr)
The North Star is the star that shines directly above the North Pole and appears never to move in the sky. Stars in Ursa Major point toward the North Star.

planets (PLAN-its)
Planets are large round objects in space that move around the Sun or another star. Eight planets move around the Sun.

plow (PLOU)
A plow is a tool used for farming that breaks up the soil before seeds are planted. Ancient people saw a plow in the stars.

quiver (KWIV-ur)
A quiver is a container for holding arrows. Callisto carried a quiver when she went hunting.

worshipped (WUR-shipt)
If something is worshipped, it is loved and respected as a god. Some ancient peoples worshipped bears.

Learn More

Books

Connelly, Bernadine. *Follow the Drinking Gourd*. New York: Simon & Schuster, 1997.

Napoli, Donna Jo. *Treasury of Greek Mythology: Classic Stories of Gods, Goddesses, Heroes, and Monsters.* Washington, DC: National Geographic, 2011.

Sparrow, Giles. *Night Sky.* New York: Scholastic, 2013.

Taylor, Carrie J. *All the Stars in the Sky: Native Stories from the Heavens.* Toronto: Tundra Books, 2006.

Web Sites

Visit our Web site for links about Ursa Major:

childsworld.com/links

Note to Parents, Teachers, and Librarians:
We routinely verify our Web links to make sure they are safe and active sites. So encourage your readers to check them out!

Index